Jesus at the heart of time
A call to
prayer

The People of
Hamilton Diocese
Celebrating the Great
Jubilee Year
2000

Jubilee
2000

Called to pray

A compilation of prayers
prepared by the people of
the Diocese of Hamilton

Published by
North Shore Publishing Inc.
Burlington, Ont.

Canadian Cataloguing in Publication Data
ISBN 1-896899-12-9

1. Prayers
2. Diocese of Hamilton
I. Title

Printed and bound in Canada

Leviticus
25: 10,12

"You shall hallow the fiftieth year
and you shall proclaim liberty throughout the
land to all its inhabitants.
For it is a jubilee;
it shall be holy to you."

Luke
4: 18-19

"The Spirit of the Lord is upon me,
because he has anointed me
to bring good news to the poor.
He has sent me to proclaim
release to the captives
and recovery of sight to the blind,
to let the oppressed go free,
to proclaim the year of the Lord's favour."

Contents

Introduction

In Christ, each one of us has been invited to be fully alive within the mystery of God's love. We have been called to free ourselves and one another from whatever holds us captive, from whatever keeps us from being embraced by our loving Creator, from whatever prevents us from embracing one another.

This time of jubilee, of entrance into another millennium, encourages us to celebrate the holy and the sacred in our ordinary lives. We are a resurrection people, a people of hope. The Spirit, who breathes new life into our being at every moment, enables us to rejoice and believe in the good news of Jesus Christ.

Many people responded to the invitation to reflect on their lives, upon Sacred Scriptures such as Ecclesiastes 3.1-8 and Ephesians 3.14-20, and to participate in the creation of this prayer book; indeed the following pages embody the hearts and thoughts of people of the Diocese of Hamilton.

Because of the limitation of space, not all submissions could be included. In order to honour all of the creativity, entries that are not found here are in a binder entitled "Jubilee 2000 Submissions". This is available at The Library at the Chancery Office, 700 King Street West, Hamilton, Ontario.

To our knowledge this book contains only original works; popular prayers may be discovered in other publications, some of which we have listed in the suggested reading section.

We are grateful for the time and energy given to this project by so many, and are encouraged by the prayerful preparation of the people of the diocese.

It is our hope that the prayers, poems, reflections and illustrations inspire you, give you hope in times of distress, light in times of darkness and surround you with the love and faith of those who walk the journey of the Christian life together.

May the Liberating God - the God of Peace - continue to bless each of us abundantly and carry us lovingly into the new millennium.

The Prayer Book Committee
Adrienne Corti
Gerry Creedon
Olga Protz
Rosanne Logel, C.S.J.
Rev. Kevin Wenkoff

Message from
The Bishop of Hamilton

Dear Friends in Christ:

The Diocese of Hamilton is preparing in many
ways to celebrate the great Jubilee of the Lord's
Birth in the year 2000. Among our preparations
is the presentation of a Jubilee Prayer Book.

People from across our diocese were invited to
submit personal prayers and responded generously.

May these ways of talking to God be a help and
an inspiration to your own life of prayer. May
they bring you the peace and joy of our Saviour
Jesus Christ.

Yours sincerely in the Lord,

A. F. Tonnos
Bishop of Hamilton

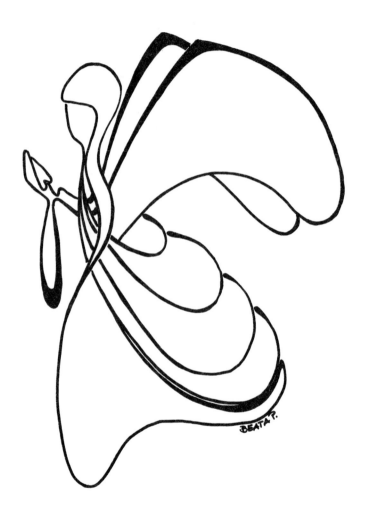

Graced Moments

"Know that I am with you always;
yes, to the end of time."   *- Matthew 28.20*

JUBILEE

Jesus, come into our hearts as we prepare
for the new millennium.

Unite all Christians so they may all be one.

Be our guide in our deliberations
and help us reach full communion.

Inspire in all the faithful a true longing
for holiness and personal renewal.

Liberate us from our brokenness
and free the oppressed from their afflictions.

Enrich our hearts, lips and hands
with faith, hope and charity.

Enlighten our understanding
and lead us to the fullness of Christian life.

Amen.

Margaret
Kraemer

Sacred
Heart
Parish
Walkerton

INTO YOUR HANDS

Into your hands, my Father,
I commit this newborn day,
depending on your mercy
each step along the way.

Into your hands, dear Jesus,
I place this life of mine,
that every waking moment
may reveal your love divine.

Into your hands, sweet Spirit,
I dedicate each hour,
for your leading and direction,
and your almighty power.

Honoria A.
Groves

Church of the
Nazarene
Oakville

With great anticipation,
this child of yours now stands,
to see your plan unfolding,
for this day is in your hands.

A NEW WAY OF PRAYING

Without the Thee's and Thou's of my youth
it's hard to know, Jesus,
if I am really praying.

I try, but the words don't seem to come.
My mind races about;
How do I start?

It seems odd to say, "Hi Jesus, it's me."
My life is a muddle:
I just run all day.

Rita
Halpin

Sacred Heart
Parish
Walkerton

But, when I sit quietly with you,
and your love fills my heart,
then I know, Jesus, I'm really praying.

ABBA, FATHER

Theresa
Goodale

St. Patrick
Parish
Burlington

He leaned down to pick me up.
As I reached up to him
the beard was soft…
framing the gentle smile,
the eyes loving me, accepting me,
unconditionally so.
He lifted me high,
the ground beneath me receding.
He held me securely,
next to the warmth of his heart.
And from my new perspective with him
everything looked new.
I could find my way now
because he carried me.

WALKING WITH GOD

Submitted in
memory of the
author,
Christine
Reinelt
who died in
August, 1990

St. Dominic
Parish
Oakville

I am now granted my walk in peace with God.
Together, hand in hand,
he will show me his kingdom.
His love will envelop me like the stars at night.
Like a mother he will cradle me in tenderness.
Like a father he will guide me on my way.
Like a sister he will share companionship.
Like a brother he will protect me.

Your Words, Lord, are Spirit and Life

I sit here, listening to your voice,
your longing for my love.

Here I am, Jesus!
You call, oh so many times - unceasingly.

Here I am, Jesus!
Your voice, your touch - so different:
tender, harsh, gentle, searing the soul,
pulling me out of myself,
ever calling forth my love,
to become one with you.

It is painful.
Often, I cannot see beyond the moment:
blindness, my wants, my pleasures,
my pride - sin.
Once again, your voice!
"Come to me...Come with me...
Follow. See, I go before you. Fear not."

Here I am, Jesus,
following - yet constantly stopping to gaze,
to enjoy, to collect little treasures -
to please only myself.

Oh, so many distractions
which take me away from you.

Roy
Boucher,
OMI

St. Joseph
Hospital
Hamilton

Ah, your voice!
"Come my child;
behold your beloved!"
Here I am, Jesus.
Take me, lead me.

17

Prayer for Discernment and Grace

Heavenly Father,
you are calling us into a deeper covenant.
In gratitude we accept the gift of your love.
We desire to discover the vision you have for us.
Show us how to live this covenant with you,
with each other and with everyone we meet.

Jesus Christ,
you are leading us on a faith journey.
In hope we await your return in glory.
We want to know you and trust you more.
Let your gentle presence among us
dispel our fears and protect us.

Holy Spirit,
you are forming us into a community.
In joy we embrace your righteousness.
We pray for your wisdom and your peace
to live in unity.
Teach us to be humble, gentle, patient,
and to bear with each other in love.

Louis
Cote

Blessed
Sacrament
Parish
Kitchener

ON THE JOURNEY OF MY LIFE

My loving God and Father,
how gently your love has unfolded
on the journey of my life.

As a youth, you knew my rebellious ways,
and yet you loved me more.
I carelessly travelled the roads of my life,
alone, I thought.
But you were my constant companion.

Even as I did not know the pain I caused,
you knew how much I would come to love you.
Persistently your voice called to me,
and I finally heard and answered.

Now my joy in you is endless.
Daily we walk together, hand in hand,
and I look forward to our meeting in heaven.

Anonymous

Holy
Rosary
Parish
Burlington

THE RECITAL: A CELEBRATION OF GOD'S GRACE

Backstage bedlam as nervous dancers clamber
for costumes,
last minute details demand attention:
a tuck in a tutu, a stitch in a stocking, a prayer
on the lips.

Anxious choreographers rehearse...
one more time,
urgent cues whispered from the wings.

Suddenly...
The scene erupts in a cavalcade of colourful
costumes!
Dozens of dancers flitting across the stage,
a bevy of butterflies brandishing God's beauty.

Dozing dads awake sleepishly from
their drowsing,
scolding moms elbow them sharply,
smiling all the while.

And now...a solo...a lone dancer
dwarfed by the enormity of the stage,
vulnerable...utterly alone...yet,
defiant in her will to excel.

Paul
Hureau

A stifled grimace, a captivating smile,
a pointe held in triumph!

St. Raphael
Parish
Burlington

Then...the grand finale...the entire troupe...
flowing in unison,
aspiring ballerinas dancing life's dream.

A DANCER'S PRAYER

Brother Jesus, your face was once before us,
your feet once touched the earth in journey,
your hands healed our bodies by their gestures,
your voice echoed in our hearts
through the movement of your love.

Now our bodies long to exult in your presence,
the presence of love for your people.

We respond to your voice.
We move to your beckoning.
All that is spirit is reality.

Make us your holy hands, holy feet,
holy faces, holy bodies.
May ours truly be a dance of your desire.
With you our dance will create holy ground.

Then the mystery which is the holy ground
of our brothers and sisters,
the holy ground that is each heart's
unique journey,
may indeed know complete intimacy with you,
O Lord.

Amen.

Colleen
Vandeven

St. Pius X
Parish
Brantford

Prayers of Young People

"Let the little children come to me,
and do not stop them;
for it is to such as these
that the kingdom of God belongs."

- Mark 10.14

A TEENAGER'S PRAYER

Thank you for giving us life on earth.
It is a pleasure to be alive
even at times when it seems our life
is caving in on us.

Help us to do the right thing
as young teenagers,
as we face dating, new friends,
and choices about future careers.
As we grow older,
help us to choose our life partner.

If we are blessed with children,
God, help us to raise them properly,
so that they are happy and safe.
As we watch our children grow older,
help us to be good and healthy grandparents.

Jennifer
Matic

St. Mary
Secondary
School
Kitchener

And at the time of our death,
help us to reflect on our life
as a positive and wonderful experience.

Amen.

A Jubilee Prayer

Dear Jesus,
you have taken good care of your people.
I am truly looking forward
to your coming again!

I will try to be more faithful to you.
I have tried to keep my Confirmation promise.
Please look after my family and friends.
I hope that you will continue
to take such good care of us
for another 2000 years.

Love, Tyler.

Tyler
Wilson

St. Mark
School
Burlington

A Morning Prayer

I wake up in the morning, God,
to birds chirping and the sun shining.
Every day I take this for granted.
I don't stop to say, "Thank you".
Help me not to forget
that you gave me such a wonderful day.

Thank you, God.

Amen.

Michele
Missere

St. Joseph
School
Fergus

A Child's Prayer

God,
teach us to care for and to respect others
and their feelings.
Help us to control our anger
and be kind to each other.
Make us understand that everyone is different
and special in their own way.
Help us not to tease each other.
God, help us to make peace!

K.Q.

St. Dominic
School
Oakville

A Disciple's Prayer

God, the Father Almighty,
you lovingly created all people in your image.
You gave up your only Son
so that we may be with you in heaven.

As the disciples of your Son, Jesus,
left all they had to become his followers,
may we too give up and leave behind
all the things in our lives
which are not necessities,
so that we may become closer to you
in the next millennium.

Danielle

Grade 8,
St. Gabriel
School
Burlington

We ask this through Christ our Lord,
who reigns for ever with you
and the Holy Spirit.

Amen.

GRADE ONE PRAYERS

God, I love you.
How are you doing?
I hope you are doing fine.
Thank you for my family
and thanks for everybody
and thanks for me.
Please help me to stop being bad.
I wish there weren't bad people around.
I wish everybody was nice.
- *Sean*

Thank you for everything you made.
Thank you for the kind people.
Can you change people's hearts
with more love?
- *Amanda*

Thank you, you are a good person.
Thank you for letting me live
and giving me a good family.
Thank you for changing the flowers
into different colours.
- *Danielle*

God, I love you.
- *Jessi*

I love you, God.
How do you do?
How is heaven?
Can you change cats into dogs?
Thank you for putting us on the land.
Thank you for dogs.
Thank you for our friends.
- *David*

St. Dominic
School
Oakville

A GRADE ONE CLASS PRAYER

Thank you, heavenly Father,
for our families,
our sisters and brothers,
our moms and dads,
our grandmas and grandpas.

Thank you, heavenly Father,
for things in the world
like trees and grass,
flowers and the sky,
sun and rain.

Thank you, heavenly Father,
for living creatures,

like snakes and hamsters,
lions and dogs,
fish and birds.

Grade
One
Class

Holy
Rosary
School
Burlington

Rob
Nagy

Holy
Rosary
School
Burlington

RECONCILIATION

Sacred, Holy,
Healing, Blessing, Renewing,
Cleansing our souls.
FORGIVE.

AN INVITATION TO THE LORD

Please Lord,
let your Holy Spirit into my life.
Every day I am faced with temptations.
I need strength.

I see many evils; I am blind to good.
I need faith.

I have been hurt and deceived;
I need to forgive.

Marc B. and
Christi S.

OAC,
Notre Dame
Secondary
School
Burlington

I walk alone
seeing no hope, only despair.
Give me the strength to continue.
Give me faith to guide me,
and forgive those who have wronged me.

Please, Lord, I need your love.

DEAR LORD

Luke
Hillyer

St. Mary
Secondary
School
Owen Sound

Dear Lord,
please help me to understand
my purpose in life.
Help me to understand who I am.
Help me to find direction in my life
and teach me how to take the first steps.

Amen.

EVER-PRESENT GOD

When I was mad at life, you were always there.
When I needed someone to talk to
I could always count on you,
Friend.

When I wanted to walk,
you would walk with me.
You never complained
and you never thought about yourself,
Saviour.

When I needed a laugh,
you always laughed with me.
When I wanted to cry
you always comforted me,
God.

Samantha
Kang

St. Mary
Secondary
School
Owen Sound

Thank you for being there
and thank you for showing me that you care.
I will always look up to you,
my friend, my Saviour, my God.

Amen.

Matt
Allemang

Holy
Rosary
School
Burlington

CONFIRMATION

A new sensation:
growing, learning, following,
a part of God,
God's Kingdom.

POURQUOI?

Seigneur, pourquoi est-ce que notre monde
est comme ça?
L'injustice existe dans tous les pays,
Et beaucoup de personnes sont toujours
maltraitées.
Le racisme existe à tous les coins du monde,
Et entre les races il n'y a pas d'équalité.
Seigneur, pourquoi est-ce que les personnes
ne peuvent pas vivre en paix?
Ils sont toujours en guerre,
les gens se tuent les uns les autres.
Avec notre technologie et notre richesse
pourquoi est-ce qu'il y a de la pauvreté?
Pourquoi Seigneur,
pourquoi est-ce qu'il y a tant de problèmes?

Helder
Ribeiro

Cathedral
High School
Hamilton

Why?

*Lord, why is our world like this? Injustice
exists in every country, and an abundance of
people are always mistreated. Racism exists
in all corners of the world, and between the
different races there is no equality. Lord,
why can people not live in peace? They are
always at war, killing one another. With our
technology and our richness, why is there
poverty? Why Lord, why are there so many problems?*

AN EASTER REFLECTION

Frank
Muretic

St. Mary
Secondary
School
Kitchener

As I sit here on Easter Sunday with my
family and friends, rejoicing at the feast,
I wonder about those people who are less
fortunate, like the people in Haiti. I wonder
if they are spending time with their families
or just looking for food to survive. I think
of the people of East Timor: they are
probably hiding from people and just hoping
to survive for this day. So, God, please
guide these people to a better and fortunate life.

Un Monde Uni

Seigneur Jésus,
Aide-nous à créer un monde plein de paix et
de joie pendant
que nous attendons l'arrivée du nouveau
millénaire.

Que les guerres, le racisme et la haine
terminent,
alors que nous apprenons à aimer nos voisins
et aussi nos ennemis.

Que tout le monde soit uni
dans la bataille contre les souffrances des
pauvres
et des affamés autour du monde
et dans nos propres quartiers.

Aide-nous à entrer dans le nouveau millénaire en
paix,
dans un monde uni dans l'amour du Christ.

Amen.

Rita
Matos

Cathedral
High School
Hamilton

A World United

Lord Jesus, help us to create a world filled
with peace and happiness, as we await the
arrival of the new millennium. May all wars,
racism, and hatred come to an end, as we
learn to love our neighbours and our enemies
as well. May we all unite in the battle against
the suffering of the poor and hungry around
the world and in our own neighbourhoods.
Help us to enter the new millennium in peace,
in a world united in Christ's love. Amen.

FOR THE POOR AND HUNGRY

Sometimes I get so mad at you, God,
because I want to see and hear you.
And sometimes I don't think you are here
because there are so many people
who are poor and hungry.
So I ask my mom,
and she says you are helping them.
I just don't see it.

Thank you, God,
for watching over the poor and hungry.
I would like to ask you something.
Could you give the poor and hungry
a little more food
and make sure they have a roof
over their heads?

I am sorry for not always giving food
to the food bank,
because I have so many things.
I praise you for the things you have given me
and for giving everyone forgiveness.
I love you.

Amen.

Student

St. Agatha
School
St. Agatha

REMEMBERING GOD

You love me so much,
yet sometimes I forget
just how much you love me.

My life is filled with other things to do
and in my busy day
I forget to make time for you -
on the bus ride to school, or at home,
or even at lunch -
so that we can talk.

Sarah McNeil

Grade 9, St. Mary Secondary School Kitchener

You know me better than anyone else
and you always have my best interests in mind,
so, when I have problems, I will come to you.
Help me to remember you
and make you a bigger part of my life.

Amen.

PRAYER FOR THE DISABLED

God, heavenly ruler of the universe,
as you healed the blind man's eyes
at Bethsaida,
help us to respect
and to take care
of the disabled of this world.

John Bourbonniere

St. Gabriel School Burlington

We ask this through Jesus Christ, our Saviour
who lives and reigns with you, and the Holy
Spirit.

Amen.

SEIGNEUR, AIDE-MOI

Seigneur, j'ai peur de la vie,
je me réveille chaque matin
et je désire réussir dans ma vie,
mais j'ai besoin de ton amour.

J'ai mille questions et
je n'ai pas de réponses.
Je veux être utile et aider le monde
mais quand j'essaie je ne vois
pas de différence
dans le monde.

Les gens de pouvoir
semblent des machines,
mais je crois que toi,
tu connais tout et je suis aveugle.

Marta
Soltys

OAC,
Cathedral
High School
Hamilton

Je te demande de m'aider
et d'être avec moi tout le temps.
Surveille-moi et aide-moi à
être une bonne personne.

Amen.

Lord, Help Me

Lord, I am afraid of life. I wake up each
morning wanting to succeed in life, but I
need your love. I have a thousand questions
and I have no answers. I want to be useful and
help the world but when I try, I don't see any
difference in the world. People of power seem
like machines, but I believe that you, you know
all and I am blind. I ask you to help me and to
be with me always. Watch over me and help
me to be a good person.

In Thanksgiving

Dear God,
you gave us life to live,
you gave us air to breathe,
you gave us light to see,
you gave us food to eat and water to drink,
you gave us darkness to sleep,
you gave us snow for Christmas,
and summer for golf and other sports,
and all of us, from the bottom of our hearts
thank you for giving us your life
for ever and ever.

Amen.

Brent
McDonald

St. Mary
Secondary
School
Owen Sound

Thanksgiving for Creation

As the breeze gently rustles through the trees,
I thank you.
As the rain sprinkles softly about the earth,
I thank you.
When the sun kisses the face
of the outside world,
I thank you.
As each living thing creeps
over the earth softly,
I thank you.
As the flowers bloom,
birds gently sing and soar,
I thank you.
As each eyelid flutters open
to a new life brought forth,
I thank you.
Creator of all beauty, seen and unseen,
I thank you,
You have made all things divine:
I thank you.

Beth
Edwards

St. Mary
Secondary
School
Kitchener

37

Seasons
of Life

"When I was a child, I spoke like a
child. I reasoned like a child; when I
became an adult, I put an end to
childish ways. And now faith, hope
and love abide, these three; and the
greatest of these is love."

- 1 Corinthians 12.11,13

THE EBB, THE FLOW

A blue sky fades,
the old spirit escapes,
as the final hour of contemplation
closes in on the final act
of the creator's latest show.

The sands of time have vanished,
images of the past decades.
Some battles lost; but many battles won
because humankind felt the assurance
of "I am with you always".

Eileen J. Brow

Regina Mundi Hamilton

Tomorrow, another landscape,
other feelings, other adventures.
Optimistically, we greet the new millennium.
We'll strive for more peace, less war.
The strife's not over, again, just begun.

AS WE PREPARE

O Lord, as we prepare ourselves for Jubilee 2000,
help us to show more love and compassion
towards others.

In being more caring Christians,
we pray that the Holy Spirit
will truly prepare our hearts
to celebrate the joy of the next millennium.

Barb Vyhnal

As we continue to read the scriptures,
may we reflect on them more seriously
to fully understand the messages they contain.

Sacred Heart Parish Walkerton

Please continue to guide us
as we follow in your footsteps.

We ask this through Christ our Lord. Amen.

A Senior's Prayer

Here I am, Lord, a weary senior.
You have dwelt in my heart
through all the stages of my life,
with all its joys and sorrows.
I have seen wars, depressions,
assassinations, racism, violence,
abuse, and family breakdown.
Sometimes in dark despair,
I closed my heart to your love,
then begged forgiveness and,
in your mercy, you forgave.
I thank you for your blessings.

Because of your great love
for your people here on earth,
this world has evolved
with all its modern technology.
As we prepare for the third millennium,
I pray that your peace
may descend on our troubled world.

Jean A.
Pilla

Holy
Rosary
Parish
Burlington

Unite your people, Lord,
so that we may work together in harmony
under your guidance
and be pleasing in your sight.

Lord hear my prayer.

41

Be With Me, Lord

Dear Lord,
please be with me always,
to watch over me,
to guard me, to guide me, and protect me,
to give me strength, to give me courage,
to give me wisdom, to give me knowledge,
to give me patience,
to give me understanding.

Amen.

*Michael
Oberholzer*

Our Lady of
Lourdes Parish
Waterloo

Calm Our Hearts

Blessed Mother, precious light,
promised dawn of sin's dark night,
with your gentle touch please guide us;
as we journey, walk beside us.

Lives of turmoil, lives of haste,
hours so filled, days gone to waste - -
interrupt our busy days,
give us pause to give God praise.

Now the hour, now the place,
let us ever seek His grace.
Calm our hearts through passing years,
to watch with Christ as heaven nears.

*Tom
Kelly*

St. Matthew
Parish
Oakville

A PRAYER TO MARY, OUR MOTHER

Hear us Mother as we kneel:
for your protection we appeal.
Bless us as we begin our day,
guide us safely on our way.

Hear us when we feel forsaken,
when with grief we're overtaken.
Help us say "Thy will be done",
guide us as you did your Son.

Hear us now because we know
many of us here below
forget to trust in God in all we do.
Guide us to keep our faith
both strong and true.

Hear us Mother when our life
on earth is done,
Intercede for us with God your Son.
Thank him for the life
and joys we know,
guide us to eternal life with you.

S. McCabe

*Sacred
Heart
Parish
Kenilworth*

QUIET SOLACE

Quiet beginnings
arise each new day again,
in full splendour,
the rich review of yesterday.

Breathless hope,
unsurpassable peace of God,
instill new life within us.

Let winter's bloom of perfection
hold us upright
with watchful eyes for Beauty's
every nook and crevice.

Let each of us surrender peacefully
in our life's scurry of events and thoughts.

Captivate us, Lord,
and hold us gently in your embrace.
Touch us softly.

Some holdings remain peaked within us,
while others are erased.

Let your fresh anointing fall upon us
like heavenly perfume.

Renew us in the rapture
of your precious love.
Let us continue to hold you
in our memories and hearts,
most cherished and precious
pearl of grace.

Carol
Gallant

St. Michael
Parish
Oakville

VOCATION

Eons have passed,
ages have come.
Here in this moment,
you are the one.

Sleepy-eyed child,
roused from your rest,
the love that is waiting
you hardly could guess.

- Wake, O Wake! -

The darkness, not knowing,
you've stumbled from bed.
Faith has just entered,
you've yet to be led.

The struggles, the pain?
That's just you yawning,
stretching and straining,
yet to be fed.

The banquet is ready,
your place is there.
My child, I love you.
Why are you scared?

Eat from my table,
drink of my blood.
Grow strong in my spirit.
O child of my love.

I am with and within you.
You're armed for your journey.
Your companions are around you.
Yes, they are many.

In this age
you are meant to be
a revelation
of my glory.

*M. C.
Janossy*

Sacred
Heart
Parish
Walkerton

I Want To Be Me

I want to be me,
no one to compare with, no one to please.
I want to say what is on my mind,
without some saying "Catch up with the time."

I want to keep an open mind,
and my heart as pure as gold.
I don't want to become
vindictive and cold.

Why should I change the ways I have,
when all I want is to be me.
I'm not anyone else, I am unique.
I do have my faults, I will admit.

Life is so short,
life is so sweet,
so why become someone else when
God gave me, me.

LA CROIX

Un symbole de bois de ma confiance en toi
Que je porte autour de mon cou
Me fait penser à toi toujours.
Je sais que je n'oublierai jamais.

Ton amour éternel
Que je conserve dans mon coeur
Comme je chéris tous les jours!
Je sais que nous ne nous séparerons jamais.

Quand je vois une croix de bois
À sa place sur le mur
Cela me rappelle le jour que
Tu as fait ta chute mais aussi le jour que
Tu es réssuscité.
Quand tu reviendras je suis
très sûre que tu me prendras avec toi
Parçe que j'aurai toujours porté ma croix!

Magenta
Chernets

Cathedral
High School
Hamilton

The Cross

A wooden symbol of my faith in you hangs
around my neck, makes me always think
of you. I know that I will never forget that
everlasting love of yours to keep deep
inside my heart. How I cherish each day;
I know that we'll never part. When I see
a wooden cross hung upon the wall,
it reminds me of the day you rose, as well as
the time you experienced your fall. When
you come again I am sure you will take me
along with you, because I have carried my
own cross always strong and true.

THE SEASONS OF DAILY LIFE

Oh, long, long winter,
freeze over our unsureness,
that we may have rest
from all our anxieties.

Oh, longed-for-spring,
warm sun that melts the snow,
melt away
our feelings of inadequacy.

Oh, promised heat of summer,
cause the love, patience and silence
deep within us
to grow like no growing season before.

*Kelly Anne
Mantler*

*St. Gregory
Parish
Cambridge*

Oh, carefree days of autumn,
take away all that hinders wholesome growth,
keeping the roots of our life nourished
deep within the light of all life.

MY SON AND I

Father, I pray so that
the love that I have for my son
and the love that my son has for me
grows every day

*John
Manuel
Larrabure*

in you,
with you,
and for you,

*St. Michael
Parish
Oakville*

we in you and you in us.

Amen.

48

JESUS, YOU'RE THE SAME TODAY

Jesus, you're the same today
as you were in Galilee and for all eternity.

Two thousand years ago, Lord,
you were born a man to save us, and,
Immortal God, you stayed. Yes...

Jesus, you're the same today
as you were in Galilee and for all eternity.

On the cross, you died for us out of love,
for our redemption.
Risen Lord, you live today. Yes...

Jesus, you're the same today
as you were in Galilee and for all eternity.

O Lord, your healing power is at work in me
today as it was in Galilee, ...cause...

Jesus, you're the same today
as you were in Galilee and for all eternity.

Germaine
Bagot

Holy Cross
Parish
Georgetown

Alleluia, praise, honour to you,
this very day and forever, all the way, ...cause...

Jesus, you're the same today
as you were in Galilee and for all eternity.

In Times of Difficulty

"Come to me,
all you that are weary
and are carrying heavy burdens,
and I will give you rest."   *- Matthew 11.28*

TODAY'S SIMON OF CYRENE

O Lord, I am in need of a Simon today.
By your grace, power, and love within me
I have made it this far, but today
I am weakened by the constant demands.

I realize only one Simon was there for you
as you struggled with the burden of all our sins.
Yet you, with little help and a great love for us,
carried through to the end and on to victory.

Strengthen my spirit, Lord,
for my handicapped child requires so, so much.
Even the smallest task seems such a chore.
And to carry this cross today,

I am in need of a Simon, O Lord.

Kelly Anne Mantler

St. Gregory
Parish
Cambridge

LA PAIX DANS LE MONDE

Seigneur Jésus Christ
Pourquoi les guerres?
Pourquoi des affamés?
Pourquoi est-ce que nous ne nous
aimons pas?
Nous sommes tous vos enfants.
Nous sommes tous frères et soeurs
dans votre coeur.
Pourquoi est-ce que nous ne
sommes pas tous frères et soeurs
dans nos coeurs?
Pourquoi est-ce que nous ne mettons pas
nos différences de côté et
vivre en paix dans un monde
plein d'amour?

Amen.

*Paula
Gomes*

*Cathedral
High School
Hamilton*

Peace in the World

*Lord Jesus Christ, why wars? Why hunger?
Why don't we all love each other? We are
your children. We are your brothers and
sisters in your heart. Why can't we all be
brothers and sisters in our hearts? Why
don't we put our differences aside and live
in a peaceful world full of love?*

Amen.

THE LIGHT WITHIN

When all the world in stillness,
is shrouded by the night,
I have nowhere to turn to
except my inner light.

In this light I find kindness,
an understanding heart,
encompassed with forgiveness,
God, guidance does impart.

A light so full of splendour
it awes me when I see
its strength and inner glory,
so very near to me.

*Oresta
Druska*

*St. Matthew
Parish
Oakville*

The light is found within you,
in every living soul.
Release the rays of sunlight,
allow your light to glow.

JESUS

Jesus is...
the light in my darkness
the peace in my anxiety
the joy in my sorrow
the hope in my despair
the sight in my blindness
the voice in my deafness
the music in my silence
the friend in my loneliness
the comfort in my fear
the protector in my danger
the anchor in my storms
my Saviour, Redeemer, and best friend.

*Lindsay
Moore*

*St. Margaret
Mary Parish
Hamilton*

54

God Be With Me

God be in my mind,
govern and control my thoughts.
God be on my lips and
monitor my words.
Speak for me when speech is required
and hold me silent when silence is your will.
God be in my heart,
that every action may be prompted
and motivated by you.

O God the Father, my Creator,
God the Son, my Saviour,
Holy Spirit, my Protector and Provider.
Amen, Amen, Amen.

Margherita
Carmen
Clarke

St. Ann
Parish
Ancaster

Prayer for Strength

Sitting
in the sun alone,
fearing
what's ahead. Unknown.
Wondering…
Can it heal such pain?
Kneeling.
Lord, give me strength, I pray.
Listening
to the voice inside,
Knowing
his love will not die.

Zenia
Zenchuk

St. Joseph
Parish
Guelph

WALK WITH ME

Father, walk with me as I ponder new
beginnings and store them
in a very special part of my heart
- to bring out and celebrate when I need to.

Walk with me, Lord,
as I stumble down life's winding
and sometimes perilous roadways
- I cannot manage alone.

Walk with me again, please,
- when my love of self overshadows
my love for others.

Will you still walk with me, Lord,
when I seek out, yet don't always find that
elusive feeling called happiness,
when try as I may, I fail to wipe away
the tears of an unhappy child,
or warm the heart of one who is poor in spirit
- are you still there beside me?

Walk with me, Lord,
- when the pain of losing someone or
something will not let go of my heart and soul.

*Judith
Mullen*

St. Patrick
Parish
Cambridge

Most importantly, Father, walk with me
- when I reach out my hand to help another
become the person they are destined to be.
I ask you please, to walk with me - and stay
awhile.

For Ailing Mothers

Dear God who made the world so bright,
the moon and stars that shine at night,
look down on us from up above,
and take care of our first love.

We wish that you will spare her pain,
give her grace to get well again.
If you prefer to have her with you,
give us grace to bear it too.

Theresa
Garvey

Our Lady of the
Assumption
Parish
Brantford

We know that you'll decide what's best,
to give her life or give her rest.
Whatever you want, one or the other,
please take good care of our dear mother.

A Setback

Do not feel sorry for me
for you see, my setback
brought God closer to me.
I was so far away from him,
never gave a thought
that I might be offending him.
Then this happened to me
and brought me to my knees.
Now, my life is so serene,
I have a life that had never been.
I know now,
God is close to me,
and there is someone
watching over me.

Eleanor
Cunningham

St. Augustine
Parish
Dundas

DIEU, EST-CE QUE TU ES AVEC MOI?

Dans le coeur de Dieu
je veux me trouver.
Dans les moments de crainte,
de peine et de tristesse,
je veux que tu me serre dans tes grands bras.

Tu as dit que ton amour est éternel,
est-ce que c'est vrai?
Mais pourquoi le monde est tourmenté
par la guerre et
beaucoup de jeunes innocents souffrent?

Dans les moments plus terribles,
je veux un signe que tu es avec moi.

Mais j'oublie quelque chose
à chaque instant de chaque jour,
tu te places dans mon coeur,
je trouve là ton amour.

*Monika
Rejnowicz*

*Cathedral
High School
Hamilton*

Aide-moi Dieu parce que je suis ici grâce à toi,
je suis vivant pour une raison:
tu m'as donné une raison pour vivre...

Merci pour ta patience et ton amour constant.

Lord, Are You With Me?

In the heart of God I want to be found. In the moments of fear, pain, and goodness I want you, Lord, to take me in your arms and hold me. You have told us that your love is eternal; is this true? Then why is our world tormented with wars, and thousands of young innocent people are suffering? In the most horrible times of my life, I want to see again that you are with me. But something of importance has been forgotten. In each instant of every day, you place yourself in my heart. There in my heart is where I shall find your love. Please help me, Lord, for I am here because of your love and grace. I am alive today for one reason; you have given me a reason to live... Thank you, Lord, for your patience and constant love.

58

A PRAYER FOR MERCY

I had no mercy on you, Jesus
when I betrayed you with a kiss.

I had no mercy when I whipped you,
crowned you with thorns,
and made you carry your cross.

I had no mercy when
I nailed you to the cross
and saw you die,
then pierced your side with a lance.

But please, Jesus,
have mercy on me at the hour of my death.

Anonymous

University
Catholic
Community
Waterloo

RESTING

Brokenness meets Perfection,
lost finds the Way,
child runs to the Father,
I have found my Lord.

His gift to me: Love Eternal.

I rest in the Father's arms;
no words are exchanged,
yet his presence is real.
I feel cared for in his arms
I am his own - precious and lovable.

Resting in the Father's arms,
building my child-like trust,
and deepening my faith,
I lie there
free…peaceful…unafraid.

*Rev.
Dan
Cyr*

Joseph
Brant
Memorial
Hospital
Burlington

THIS DAY

As I begin to pray, please help me dear Lord to shut out the noises that surround me. I only wish to hear your voice.

Please be with me this day in good times and bad. Give me insight to do your holy will this day, the vision to see the good in the bad and to use my bad times as stepping stones rather than stumbling blocks.

Please grant me the wisdom to see what is right and what is wrong. Strengthen my faith and increase my love during this day and all tomorrows.

Give me a sense of worth and of value knowing everything comes from you. Let me be an instrument of your love and give me the ability to share your goodness with others.

I ask for inner certainty of faith to know that you are in control and that all things that happen to me this day are for my own growth.

Doreen
Juurlink

St. Matthew
Parish
Oakville

Therefore dear Lord, I place all my trust in you and ask you to lift me from my ingratitude to a state of thankfulness.

May this prayer be the link in my chain of faith, an unbreakable chain binding you and me together for all eternity.

LISE'S PRAYER

Heavenly Father, you have once again led me out of darkness. Above all, you have guided my life in ways unknown to me. In your infinite wisdom and love, you have steered me through the events of my life like a master navigator. I did not know which way I was going. I was afraid of the dark skies and stormy seas. You alone comforted me and gave me strength to hold on. I am only a passenger, you are the vessel.

Thank you for helping me to trust, even when I thought it was impossible. Thank you for letting me show mercy and kindness - even when I myself cried out for it.

What can I do now to thank you? I trust that you will give me the strength and knowledge so that every day my heart will cry out in thanksgiving to you. Help me to be an example, so that others may feel your love and mercy through me.

Lise
Dufrense

St. Matthew
Parish
Oakville

Thank you Father for your compassion, your wisdom, your mercy and your love.

STILL

I'm still here, Lord.
Are You?

Are you still within my heart?
Is that your spirit I hear
in the quiet of my soul?
Is that your love I feel
as I slowly open my mind to hear your word?
Is that your strength within me
as I struggle to do your will?

*Patricia
Blomeley-
Maddigan*

Yes! It is I, the Lord.

*Holy
Rosary
Parish
Burlington*

Yes! It is you, Lord Jesus.
You - still - in my heart, my soul, my mind.
Forever within me, your Spirit dwells,
and for that, Jesus,
I am eternally thankful.

SPIRITUALITY 2000

A spirituality based on original sin:
guilt, punishment, fear,
destroy, despise, despair,
stifle, stagnate, slowly suffocate.
I scream!.....I cannot!

A spirituality of denial and asceticism:
the old miser promises his stomach brandy
if he will just swallow the rancid rock-hard salami.
Success, my stomach! See, no need for the
reward now!
Perverse!.....I will not!

My spirituality rooted in Slavonic melancholy:
ages of oppression and exploitation,
hard work sung in a minor key,
embroidered in bright colours,
transplanted into Canadian innocence!
Dominus Deus noster, miserere!

A spirituality based on a resurrection after
crucifixion:
consolation in misery, gentleness amidst violence,
true rest in face of utter fatigue, order from chaos,
truth dominating over hypocrisy, humility
overwhelming arrogance.
I pray,.....empower me!

A spirituality in the new covenant:
no self-induced sacrifice, just growing pains,
pains that delight the lover, that intensify the love!
Ultimate consummation in Christ!
I gasp,.....overwhelm me!

A spirituality for the third millennium:
a resurrection from the crucifixion of despair,
a new covenant exuberantly fearlessly creative,
a kingdom annulling the traumas of arrogance.
With the psalmist beseeching:
we are a people who long to see your face, O Lord.

Ann Sirek
Eperjesi

St. Louis
Parish
Waterloo

A Modern Woman's Prayer to Notre Dame - Notre Mère

Notre Dame, Our Lady,
Notre Mère, Mother of us all.
You reveal to us divine love as merciful,
close by, interested in the human condition,
ready to hear human needs,
ready to respond to our requests.

You are the compassionate Mother.
I emulate you in your life as a genuine woman
whose earthly existence was a journey of faith.
You are my consoler in times of stress,
my intercessor at the side of your divine Son.

Our Lady, helper and advocate
of mothers today,
bless our children,
Sharon Marini - Buzzelli
especially N. and N...
Watch over their daily lives. Protect them.
Help them to learn, to achieve, to succeed,
St. Gabriel Parish Burlington
to prayerfully reflect.

Notre Dame, Notre Mère. Amen.

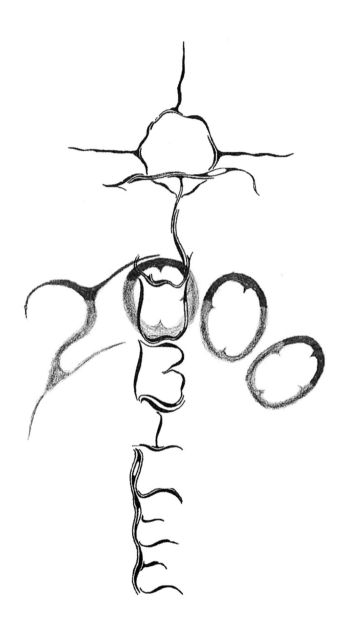

Multicultural Prayers

"...all the members of the body,
 though many, are one body, so it is
with Christ. For in the one Spirit we
were all baptized into one body - Jews
or Greeks, slaves or free - and we
were all made to drink of one Spirit."

- 1 Corinthians 12.12-13

Love One Another

"Love one another as I have loved you."

Lord this is one of the hardest things you asked of us.

We think of ourselves as number one, better than others.

Only with your help and guidance can we do as you ask.

Teach us Lord that you love everyone equally and we must too.

Colour, creed, or nationality must not make a difference.

You asked your heavenly Father to forgive your tormentors because you loved them.

All you know is love.

Help our divided world by giving us the peace that surpasses all understanding.

Joan Thomas

St. Raphael Parish
Burlington

GLORY TO GOD
(Vietnamese)

*Vinh Hang
Tran*

St. Joseph
Parish
Guelph

Vinh danh CHA Dâng toãn năng hãng có,
CHA dã tao dung dãt trõi mõt cách toãn my vã,
CHA dã sinh ra chúng con gioñg hinh anh CHA,
nhãn dúc vã thanh thién.
Xin CHA thúóng day bão cón cái,
CHA hiêu duóc thánh y cúa CHA.

Glory to God

*Glory to you God, Father almighty and
eternal, who is creator of heaven and earth,
perfect beauty. You created us in the image
of yourself, benevolent and holy. Jesus,
teach us how to understand the holy design
of God.*

69

UNIS DANS LE CHRIST

Si tout le monde travaille ensemble, nous
pouvons faire ce qui est
possible. Nous pouvons faire tout ce qui est
possible si nous ne regardons
pas nos différences. Nous ne devons pas
regarder la couleur de notre
peau, notre âge, notre hauteur, ni notre
poids. Nous devons réaliser que
nous sommes égaux. Le Christ nous a fait
réaliser notre égalité quand il
nous a raconté les paraboles. Christ, dans le
temps du Jubilé 2000 nous nous
souvenons de tout ce que Tu as fait
pour le monde. Nous sommes
plus comme une famille à cause de Ta vie.
Nous sommes reconnaissants
de t'avoir dans nos vies.

*Nadia
Fortino*

Cathedral
High School
Hamilton

United in Christ

*If everyone would work together, we could
accomplish anything possible. We can
accomplish anything if we do not look at our
differences. We must not base our
judgements on the colour of our skin, our
age, our height, or our weight. We must
realize that we are all equal. Christ made
us realize our equality when he told us his
parables. Christ, in this time of Jubilee
2000, we remember all of the things you
have done for everyone. We are more like a
family because of your life. We are thankful
to have you in our lives.*

NAAGADOOWN GMIIKON
(Ojibway)

Gizhe-mnidoo gii-miingowaa
miikon waa nagodooyeg
Ji naadmoowdwaa bemaadzijig.

Kina gmiina gzaagidwin Gzhi-minidoo
Niibnaa gego gii ngaadaan, wii-nakiitwaad
Gizhe-minidoo.

Gda kinoomage,
gda-naanogdwenmaa yaaksid.
Gda naametwaa nebood.

Gchi-piitendaagwaad maanda ezhchigeyaag.
Weweni naagaadoog gmiiknaawa.

Maawnjistoodaa gdinmemninaan.
Maanch go ezhi debwewendmaang.
Gzhi-mnidoo kina gii miingonaan
Naanagdowendmowin, zaagidwin.

*Ernestine
Proulx*

*St. Mary
Church
Cape Croker*

Kina naasaab gda ezhi bgosendaamin.
Pii nebooying ji mnadopnigyeng
Gzhi-mnidoo.

Follow Your Path

The Lord gave you a path to follow, to help all people. You give all your love to the Lord. You gave up many things to do His work. You teach, you look after the sick, you pray for the dying. The work you do is held in high regard. Follow your path carefully. Let us join our prayers together regardless of belief. The Lord gave each of us a mind and love. We all hope for the same, that when we die the Lord will accept and greet us with love.

我靈頌

設想漫長深夜,輾轉難眠
飲泣至入夢
又恐醒來迎接另一天的絕望

設想恨火焚心,意消神傷
無可理喻
到頭總成灰爐

設想無止境的貪婪
窮追達不到的願望
一如困獸,永無寧日
不外都為幻影

久候的黎明終到來
心神解脫,再無憂慮

教我能不終身感激
你的降臨,你的愛
給我帶來無比的神寧?

陳小明

S. M.
Chen

Holy
Rosary
Parish
Burlington

72

My Soul Rejoices

Imagine the endless sleepless nights
of weeping until exhaustion,
in fear of waking up
to another day of despair.

Imagine the hatred that burns from within,
consuming and destroying
beyond all reasons,
in the end leaving ashes.

Imagine the insatiable hunger
racing from one ideal to another,
restless like a caged animal,
for what other than shadows.

Then came dawn,
and freedom from all these.....

How can I help but proclaim
with continuous gratitude
for the rest of my life
the peace that you have brought
through loving enough to become one of us?

ACERCÁNDONOS AL PADRE
(Spanish)

¡Padre! Escucha nuestra oración,
haz que este movimiento de preparación
y celebración del Advenimiento de tu Hijo,
nos envuelva totalmente, renovando nuestra fe
en tí, Dios Todopoderoso.

Que nuestro ser interior se fortalezca con tu Espiritu y
nos otorgues la gracia
de acercanos más a Ti,
de vivir conforme Tú lo has establecido,
siguiendo e imitando a tu Hijo Amado,
viviendo cada instante de nuestras vidas
señidos a tu verdad y encarnados en tu amor.

Que los momentos dificiles nó nos angustien o afanen,
sino más bien nos estimúlen, nos acerquen, nos
conduzcan
a apoyarnos más en Ti...a abandonarnos en Tí,
a buscar a tu Hijo con más fuerza y decisión,
para que, con la confianza
que dá la fe en Cristo,
esperemos y actuemos conforme Tú
ya, lo has dispuesto.

Que seámos para nuestras familias
presencia permanente de tu amor y tu verdad:
y para nuestra comunidad,
fieles promotores de tu Palabra a través de nuestro
ejemplo de vida,
nuestro respeto, comprensión y solidaridad con
nuestros hermanos.

Asi, ¡Padre Eterno!
Nos unimos a la misión de tu Hijo,
a la realización de tu sueño:
Constituir a la humanidad en un solo cuerpo...tu
Iglesia,
en una sola raza...la raza humana
en una sola clase social...los hijos de Dios,
profesando, todos, un solo credo...tu amor y tu verdad.

Asi sea

*Aracely
Salazar - Clara*

Spanish
Community -
Our Lady of
Guadalupe
Kitchener

Coming Closer to Our God

*Father, hear our invocation; may this time of
preparation and celebration of the birth of your
Son involve us totally, renewing our faith in you,
Almighty God.*

*May our inner being be strengthened by your Spirit
and may you give us the grace to
be closer to you, living according to your will,
following and imitating your loving
Son, living each moment of our lives faithful to your
truth and incarnated in your love.*

*May the difficult moments not worry or distress us,
but may they motivate us, bring
us close to you, lead us to depend on you, to
abandon ourselves to you, to follow
your Son with greater conviction, so that, filled
with the trust that comes with faith
in Christ, we can hope and live according to what
you have already determined.*

*May we be a permanent presence of your love and
your truth for our families, and for
our community, faithful promoters of your word
through an exemplary life, respect,
understanding and solidarity with our brothers
and sisters.*

*And so, Eternal Father, we join in your Son's
mission, to fulfill your dream: that all
humanity be one body...your church, one race...the
human race, one social class...the
sons and daughters of God, all professing one
creed...your love and your truth. Amen.*

PAGSAMA-SAMA AT PAGKAKAISA KAY KRISTO

(Philippine Language)

Mahal no Panginoon at Ama, kami ay lubos na nagpapasalamat sa iyong minamahal na anak na si Hesus. Isinugo ninyo siya sa mundo para siya naming Manunubos at taga-pagligtas. Dahil sa kadakilaan ng inyong pagmamahal sa amin ipinagkaloob ninyo siya sa amin. Naging kaisa namin siya para kami ay maging banal at karapat-dapat na tawagin ninyong kalugod-lugod na mga anak.

Panginoon, ipinahayag ninyo ang inyong pagmamahal sa amin sa pamamagitan ng inyong anak na si Hesus. Ibinigay ninyo siya, bilang kabuuan ng inyong malaking pagpapala sa amin. Mahal na Ama, tulungan mo kaming tanggaping lubos si Kristo sa aming buhay. Mahalin siya ng lubos, Paglingkuran at Parangalan siya, sa pamamagitan ng aming mga kapatid bilang paghahanda sa pagdiriwang ng Pangalawang Milenio ng kapanganakan ni Hesus.

Isugo ninyo ang ilaw ng banal no Espiritu para damahin at pag-alabin ang mga puso ng lahat ng tao sa buong mundo. Marapatin ninyo na magkaroon ng pagsasama-sama, pagkakaisa sa pagkilala at pagdakila na si Hesus ang Hari ng lahat ng nilikha dito sa lupa at sa langit.

Turuan ninyo kami na mahalin kayo ng lubos. Sa araw-araw; kami ay gabayan sa aming paglalakbay tungo sa patuloy naming paglago sa aming pananampalataya. Pagkalooban mo kami ng lakas, upang maisakatuparan namin ng buo ang gawaing idinulot mo sa amin hang matamo ang koronang banal na ipinangako mo sa amin. Dalagnin namin ito kay Kristo ngayon at magpasawalang hanggan. Siya nawa.

Amen

Anonymous

St. Joseph
Parish
Guelph

Unity and Oneness in Christ

*Loving God and Father, we thank you for
sending your beloved Son, Jesus, to the world
as our Redeemer and Saviour. In your great love
for us, you have allowed Jesus to unite with us,
so that we would become holy and worthy to be
called your precious sons and daughters.*

*Jesus is the expression of your love for us. You
have given him for us so graciously, and in large
measure. Father, make us pure and deserving, to
receive him wholeheartedly into our lives. Help
us to love him, serve him, and please him
through our brothers and sisters as we joyfully
celebrate the second millennium of Jesus' birth.*

*Send forth the light of the Holy Spirit to touch
the hearts of people all over the world. Then
there will be unity and oneness in recognizing
Christ as the head of all creation, both in heaven
and on earth.*

*Teach us to love you more each day. Walk with
us as we continue to grow in our faith journey.
At such time that we can bring into completion
the work which you have given us, and reap the
crown of glory which you have promised. In
Jesus' name we pray. Amen*

Tratta da
LA PREGHIERA DELL'IMMIGRANTE
(Italian)

Io sono una voce di tanti uomini alienati,
Lontani dalle famiglie e divisi dal mare crudele
e maledetto,
Sul quale navigammo in terza classe
Nelle prigioni sotterranee, grandi e scure,
Delle navi che ci ninnavano
Senza mai avvicinarci alla terra promessa.

Sogno la terra riarsa dai giorni canicolari
Però desidero di ritornare ai prati inariditi
Che mi costrinsero a partire;

Di sentire le canzoni dei mietitori stanchi
Mentre ritornano dalla campagna;

Per inebriarmi ancora una volta delle fragranze
fresche
Eccitate dai boschi di pini.

Source:
The
Immigrant's
Prayer

*Anthony M.
Buzzelli*

St. Gabriel
Parish
Burlington

Mi mancano I figli; proteggili.
Rendili consapevoli del loro padre
Che é partito per preparare una vita
Impossibile sulla tua sommità sassosa e
sublime.
Aiutali a ricordarsi di me!

Ho tempo di pensare
I miei figli avranno l'istruzione che fu negata a me.
Il mio sogno si avverará in loro.

Excerpt from
The Immigrant's Prayer

*I am one voice of many estranged men, bereft
of families and separated by a cruel and
cursed sea, upon which we rode steerage in
dark cavernous dungeons of ships lulling
us no closer to the promised land.*

*I dream of the soil parched by the dog days of
summer and yet long to return to the
meager fields which forced me away;*

*To hear the reapers' weary song as they
return from the fields;*

*To be once more intoxicated by cool
fragrances whipped up by forests of pine
trees.*

*I miss my children; take care of them. Let
them know that their father has gone to
prepare a life not possible on your rocky and
sublime summit. Help them remember me!*

*I have time to think my children will have the
education denied me. My dream will be
fulfilled in them.*

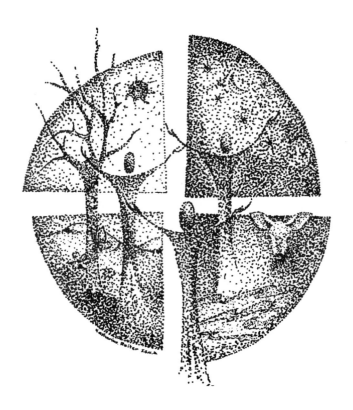

Creation

"Consider the lilies, how they grow:
they neither toil nor spin; yet I tell you,
even Solomon in all his glory was not
clothed like one of these. But if God so
clothes the grass of the field, which is
alive today and tomorrow is thrown into
the oven, how much more will he clothe
you - you of little faith!" *- Luke 12.27-28*

THE FREEDOM TO FLY

The new millennium frees us from the past
for harmony is restored and love holds fast.

As darkness lifts, the majestic sky is clear;
in the warm light we feel God's presence near.

Like birds in a nest,
unity is necessary to survive;
Respecting nature will keep creation vibrant and
alive.

The Holy Spirit comforts us
and calms our fears;
It is time to honour one another
and wipe away tears.

Louise-Ann
Caravaggio

Holiness and purity flood each Christian heart;
This time in history marks a glorious start.

Canadian
Martyrs
Hamilton

As gentle young doves lift our wings to fly,
hoping to improve the world before we die.

JUBILÉ... 2000

Ses yeux révèlent la joie
Ses mouvements le plaisir continu.
Il voit la verité, pas ce qu'il apparaît verité.

La serenité au ciel,
Les courants des rivières
Retiennent la beauté de Dieu.

C'est par son intervention que
Les aveugles peuvent voir.
C'est par son intervention que
Les malades peuvent guérir.

C'est par les bénédictions de Dieu
Qu'un jeune garçon peut rayonner d'amour.

*Charles
Agro*

*Cathedral
High School
Hamilton*

Grace à l'amour on peut donner la paix
Et la partager.
Et c'est pour ça que nous sommes Unis en Lui.

Amen

Jubilee 2000

*His eyes reveal happiness, his movements
continuous joy. He sees what is, not what
appears to be. The serenity of the sky, the flow of
the rivers hold beauty from God above. It is
through God's revelations that the blind can
see; it is through God's revelations that the
hurting can heal. It is through God's blessing
that a young boy glows with love. It is through
God's love that one can give peace to those in
need and because of this, we are united in
Christ.*

Amen

THE GIFT

You wrapped a gift, Lord, in white and gold,
and you put it under a tree.
I smiled when I saw it there,
I knew it was for me.

It looked so pretty, I left it there,
I kept it as a treasure,
I knew you loved me - how could you not?
The gift was a measure.

And then one day you called to me,
you bowed your head, you shed a tear.
"You never opened your gift," you said,
"My child, why do you fear?"

"But Lord," I said, "I want to serve you,
and I want to do your will."
I rattled on and on, until,
you raised your hand, "Be still...

"Tell my people about their Saviour,
and how I died for them,
and how my blood has washed their sins.
Turn to me, repent!

"But, Lord," I cried, "I am too shy,
and you need to make me bold."
"Open your gift, my child and see,
I already gave you gold."

Betty
Goral

St. Agatha
Parish
St. Agatha

"Look inside yourself and see,
the gift of me inside;
since the day you opened your heart to me,
I've stood right by your side."

GOD'S FACE IS

God's face is:
a sunbeam that dances,
a soft breeze that blows,
a stone in a puddle, the dew on a rose.

The laughter of children, the song of a bird,
someone who listens and lets me be heard.

A letter from someone, who lives far away,
the telephone call that helps make my day.

Invitations to dinner, with people I love,
the moon in the sky, and the coo of a dove.

Kittens and puppies, and great lions that roar,
horses and cougars, and eagles that soar.

Campfires and singsongs, and stars in the night,
fluffy white clouds, and the tail of a kite.

The old and the lonely, the sick and the lame,
the poor and the homeless,
God's face is the same.

Mountains and blue skies, and fish in the sea,
all that I know, is God's face for me.

The music of Mozart, the call of a loon,
the patter of raindrops, a mass at high noon.

*Eileen
McTeague*

*St. Mary
Parish
Owen Sound*

But the face that I search for,
and long most to see,
is the face at my centre,
the God within me.

CREED WRITTEN BY DEVELOPMENT AND PEACE

Invermera 1996

We believe in the ecological sustainability of our planet.

We believe that the needs of the poor have priority over the wants of the rich.

We do not believe that there are no alternatives to the present economic order.

We do not believe in the pursuit of individuals and corporate wealth and power at the expense of the common good.

We believe that the participation of marginalized groups takes precedence over the preservation of a system that excludes them.

We believe that our masks come off and that we can recognize the true value of life when we come into contact with the poor and marginalized.

Source:
Development
and Peace

Submitted by
*Christine
McCardell*

Blessed
Sacrament
Parish
Hamilton

We do not believe in unjust profits that are achieved by the exploitation of labour and the environment.

We do not believe that the goods of the earth were created for a select few.

We all have faith in the essential goodness of people.

We have faith in our God of justice who loves the poor.

Upon Awakening

God, I love you.
Thank you for another day of life!

I am sorry for hurting others
with my impatient words
and selfish choices.

Thank you so much for your real presence
and providence in my life,
despite my weaknesses!

Please be the inspiration this day in all
relationships.

I love you, God.

*Rev. Kevin
Wenkoff*

Church
of Our Lady
Guelph

Praise and Thanksgiving

Then he took a loaf of bread,
and when he had given thanks,
he broke it and gave it to them, saying,
"This is my body, which is given for you.
Do this in remembrance of me."
And he did the same with the cup
after supper, saying, "This cup that is poured
out for you is the new covenant
in my blood.." *- Luke 22.19-20*

DEAR JESUS

As the great Jubilee draws near,
I give my thanks to you
for all the days behind me,
as I walk towards the new.

I ask for your guidance,
in all the coming days.
Please give to me your wondrous grace
when I fold my hands to pray.

Many years have passed on by.
Regrets, I have a few,
but I'll keep looking forward,
staying close to you.

Theresa
Bowier

Sacred
Heart
Parish
Kenilworth

GRACE BEFORE MEALS

Loving God,
we are especially thankful
for the many blessings
we have received from you.

We ask for the grace of faith to see your hand
in all that touches our lives,
and glimpse your love in the people
who have crossed our paths.
We thank you for the food
we are about to share,
remembering those
less fortunate than ourselves.

Let us be open to touch others
with your love, compassion, and peace.

Amen.

Jacqueline
Schneider

St. John's
Parish
Burlington

MERCI POUR TOUT

Cher Dieu,
Merci pour tout ce que vous me donnez.

Merci pour ma mère et mon père
et pour toutes les personnes qui entrent
dans ma vie.

Merci pour mes yeux qui me permettent
de voir ta création magnifique,
et pour mon coeur
qui m'aide à voir ce qui'est vraiment important.

La vie sans amour ne vaut rien.
Alors, merci pour l'amour que vous me donnez
et pour l'occasion de la partager avec les autres.

Merci pour fournir les nécessités de la vie,
aussi bien que les luxes.
Il y a bien des personnes qui n'ont rien,
des personnes qui souffrent de faim et de
maladies.

Trouvez dans nos coeurs de les aider,
et de remplir leur vie de joie,
La joie comme vous me donnez.

Merci pour tout.

Anna
Zurek

Cathedral
High School
Hamilton

Thank you for Everything

Dear God, thank you for everything that you give me.

Thank you for my mom and my dad and all the people that enter my life.

Thank you for my eyes which allow me to see your magnificent creation, and for my heart which allows me to see what is truly important. Life without love is meaningless.

Thank you for the love that you give me, and occasions to share this love with others.

Thank you for providing me with the basic necessities of life, as well as luxuries.

There are many people who have nothing, people who suffer from hunger and disease.

Find it in our hearts to help them, and fill their lives with joy, the joy that you give me.

Thank you for everything.

YOUR SPIRIT AND LIFE

Sister Mary
Joanette
Paleczny,
S.S.N.D.

St. Louis
Convent
Waterloo

Jesus, flood my soul with your mind, your
heart, your attitudes, that in every thought I
think, every word I speak, every action I
perform, every decision and opinion of mine, I
do the Father's will as you would do it
- loving God, with my whole heart; and loving
my neighbour as myself. Amen.

OPEN TO GOD'S SPIRIT

God of fulfillment,
you promised through your Son
the Spirit of Truth,
to bring us closer to you.

May the same Spirit
that was poured out at Pentecost,
continue to guide the Church
as we await the renewal
of the Great Jubilee Feast.

May we always be open to the Spirit,
and attentive to your call,
that we may be empowered,
to share and live out
the mysteries of our faith.

Joel
Henderson

St. James
Anglican
Dundas

We ask this through Jesus Christ
our Lord, who is alive and active
in the hearts of the faithful.

Amen.

JESUS IN SCRIPTURES

Jesus strengthen our faith in you
as we encounter you personally
through the words of Scripture.

Let your light shine upon us and,
like the disciples of old,
we will proclaim your words and deeds.

Strengthen and embolden us
so that we may courageously love others
to our full capacity.

Michael
Finoro

St. Joseph
Parish
Guelph

Through the intercession of the Holy Spirit,
let us love one another wholeheartedly,
thereby achieving our mission on earth.

HIS MOST HOLY FACE

I am the face of hope,
that shines before you now,
in brilliance and in majesty.
Before me come and bow.

I am the face of mercy,
that beckons you to come,
with contrite heart and simple words -
Do not cry, my cherished one.

Vilia Milic

Regina
Mundi
Parish
Hamilton

For I have known you always,
as my father has, above;
and in my heart I enfold you -
for I am the face of love.

THANKSGIVING

In our world of wonder,
we are blest.
We thank you Lord.

In Canada, a peaceful country,
we are blest.
We thank you Lord.

In our loving families,
we are blest.
We thank you Lord.

In our ever-growing faith,
we are blest.
We thank you Lord.

Rita
Sheridan

St. Mary
Immaculate
Parish
Elora

Diocesan Prayers for the Jubilee

1996- 2000

We are Church
United in Christ
Open to the Spirit
Called to Conversion
Invited to the Feast

The Jubilee 2000 logo

The logo for the preparations and celebration of Jubilee 2000 in the Diocese of Hamilton was designed by Joseph Roy, a liturgical artist.

The design incorporates the three persons of the Blessed Trinity and the People of God, and expresses the central mysteries of our  Christian faith. Through the waters of baptism the Church is brought to birth in every age. The People of God are signed with the cross of Jesus Christ in their baptism and become living members of his Body. It is through our share in the death and resurrection of Jesus Christ that we are reconciled to God and to one another. The hands of God the Father are always extended in healing and blessing over the human race; God never ceases to call the Christian people to authentic conversion.

The Holy Spirit - in the form of a dove - continues to lead and direct the work of the Church for the salvation of the world.

The logo calls all Christian people to deepen and celebrate their faith in preparation for the celebration of the great Jubilee in the year 2000 and the new millennium of Christianity.

1996 - WE ARE CHURCH

O God,
you have given us Jesus, your Son
as a light for every nation on earth.

In him, you revealed your love
and made us your own.

As we prepare to celebrate
the second millennium of Christ's birth,
pour out upon all people
the abundant gifts of your Holy Spirit.

Open our ears to listen to your word.
Teach us to serve one another
with love and respect.
Lead us on the path to unity
with all our brothers and sisters in Christ.

Renew the faith of your Church today
that we may celebrate your wonderful deeds
and bring your light to people everywhere.

We ask this through Christ our Lord.

1997 - UNITED IN CHRIST

Eternal God,
in the fullness of time
you sent your Son,
born of the Virgin Mary,
to be the source of life
for all the world.

Through the waters of baptism
you have made us your people,
and members of Christ's body,
the Church.

As we prepare to celebrate
the great jubilee of Christ's birth,
empower us with your Spirit,
that we may faithfully proclaim
the good news
of our salvation in Christ.

Remove from our hearts
all that divides us,
and direct our steps on the path to unity
with all Christians.
May we profess one faith
and serve you
in our sisters and brothers.

We ask this through Christ Our Lord.

1998 - OPEN TO THE SPIRIT

Eternal God,
by the breath of your Spirit
creation dawned.
By the power of your Spirit
your people are united
in the bond of love.
By the movement of your Spirit
our hearts are filled
with wonder and delight.

May we recognize and welcome
the abundant gifts of your Spirit
at work in your people today.

As we approach a new millennium
of Christian faith,
deepen our commitment
to the Gospel way of life,
and empower us with a firm desire
to work for unity
with all who believe in you.

May our faithful witness to the Gospel
renew in the hearts of all people
a sure and certain hope
for the coming of your kingdom.

We ask this through Christ our Lord.

1999 - CALLED TO CONVERSION

God and Father of all,
in your infinite love
you created us to reveal your glory.

Each time we have sinned
and turned away from you,
you have called us back
to the tender embrace of your love.

In the fullness of time,
you sent Jesus to be our Redeemer,
and through his death and resurrection
you have reconciled us to yourself.

As we prepare for the great Jubilee
of Christ's birth among us,
may we heed his prayer
that all may be one.

Give us courage to stand against evil
and to choose always the path of life.
Teach us to forgive one another.
Inspire us to reach out with compassion
to our brothers and sisters in need.
Renew within us a deeper commitment
to the works of justice and peace.

We ask this through Christ our Lord.
Amen.

2000 - INVITED TO THE FEAST

Praise and glory to you, O God!
In every generation
you reveal your loving kindness.
In the fullness of time
you sent your Son into the world
to announce the good news of salvation
and the promise of eternal life.

Unite our voices in joyful praise
with the heavenly choirs
who hailed his birth.
As we celebrate the great jubilee,
may we be one with the saints of every age
in bearing faithful witness to Christ.

At the dawning of this new millennium,
pour out your Spirit of justice,
peace and unity upon all people.
As we face the future,
refresh our faith, increase our hope
and deepen our love for one another.

Through our celebration of this jubilee year,
draw all people to the eternal feast
of your kingdom.
We ask this through Christ our Lord.

Suggested Reading

Aiken, Nick, *Prayers for Teenagers*. Marshall Pickering (Harper Collins) London, 1989. A collection of prayers from young Christians throughout the UK.

Bell, John A., *He Was in the World*. Wild Goose Publications, The Iona Community, The Cromwell Press, Melsham, Wiltshire, 1995. Meditations for Public Worship - A Collection of 25 meditations covering a range of personal, pastoral, and biblical themes for use in congregational worship or in smaller assemblies such as prayer groups.

Bergan, Jacqueline Syrup and Shwan, S. Marie, *Taste and See*. St. Mary's Press, Christian Brothers Publications, Winona, Mass., 1996. Prayer Services for Gatherings of Faith.

Campbell, Camille, *Teresa of Avila*. Bear & Company, Sante Fe, New Mexico, 1985. Meditations from the Book of the Mansions (or Interior Castle) which Teresa wrote during her struggles. Teresa gives a complete map through her own journey, thus helping readers with their journeys.

Ford, J. Massyngbaerde, *Welcoming Heaven*. Twenty-Third Publishing, Mystic, Connecticut, 1990. Prayers and Reflections for the Dying and Those Who Love Them - an expression of faith, courage, and peace.

Gabriel, Edward Francis, *From Many, One*. Ave Maria Press, Notre Dame, Indiana, 1995. Praying our Rich and Diverse Cultural Heritage - A collection of prayer services for morning, midday, evening, and night that remembers and celebrates the various North American communities which have suffered bigotry and oppression.

Gallagher, Blanche, *Teilhard de Chardin*. Bear & Company, Sante Fe, New Mexico, 1988. A reflective and meditative collection of Teilhard's Essays.

Gatelely, Edwina, *Psalms of a Laywoman*. Claretian Publications, Chicago, 1981. Edwina's autobiographical prayer-poems relate the milestones - joyful, sorrowful, and glorious which she has passed in her struggle to develop lay missionary activity.

Halpin, Marlene, *Imagine That!* Brown Roa Publishing Media, Dubuque, Iowa 1982. In a series of exercises, Marlene invites us to use our imaginations to come to a deeper knowledge of ourselves and God.

Hays, Edward, *Prayers for a Planetary Pilgrim*. Forest of Peace Books Inc., Easton, Kansas, 1989. A personal manual for prayer and ritual - A global way of praying that provides a pattern for prayer using morning and evening prayers for each of the four seasons of the year.

Holmes, Urban T., *Praying with the Family of God*. Winston Press, Minneapolis, Minnesota, 1979. Selections for children from The Book of Common Prayers. A story illustrating the theme introduces each service. A commentary follows.

Johnson, Ann, *Miriyam of Nazareth*. Ave Maria Press, Notre Dame, Indiana, 1984. Woman of Strength and Wisdom - Among the reflections on Mary are a set of magnificats, beyond the resurrection, ascension, pentecost, and "dormition".

Johnson, Ann, *Miriyam of Jerusalem*. Ave Maria Press, Notre Dame, Indiana, 1991. Teacher of Disciples - Magnificats on such themes as justice, healing, fidelity, and holiness, the teachings of Jesus.

Koch, Carl. ed., *Dreams Alive: Prayers by Teenagers*. St. Mary's Press, Winona, Min., 1991.

Loder, Ted, *Guerrillas of Grace*. Lura Media, San Diego, California, 1984. Prayers for the Battle - A collection of prayers of listening, thanks, praise, comfort, commitment, seasons, and holidays.

Mossi, John and Toolan, Suzanne, *Canticles and Gathering Prayers*. Saint Mary's Press, Christian Brothers Publications, Winona, Minnesota, 1985. A collection of prayers of thanksgiving and meal prayers suitable for the ecumenical Christian community. Their informality, variety, and adaptability to many situations expand their usefulness.

National Liturgical Office, *Prayers for the Jubilee 2000*. Concacan Inc., Ottawa, Ontario, 1997. A book of resources for use in Canada during the three years of preparation for the third millennium and for the year 2000.

National Liturgical Office, Canadian Conference of Catholic Bishops, ed. *Family Book of Prayer*. Concacan Inc., Ottawa, Ontario, 1983. The prayers and suggestions in this book of family prayer come to us from across the centuries.

Office of Religious Education, Diocese of Hamilton, 1981. *Lord Hear Our Prayer*. Various kinds of prayer, basic prayers for all occasions.

Reehorst, Jane, *Guided Meditations for Children*. Brown Publishing, Dubuque, Iowa, 1991. How to teach children to pray using scripture.

Schaffran, Janet and Kozak, Pat, *More Than Words*. Meyer Stone Books, Oak Park, Illinois, 1986. Prayer and Ritual for Inclusive Communities - A collection of 30 multi-cultural, justice-oriented, inclusive prayer services along with a source book for developing your own inclusive prayers and rituals.

Uhlein, Gabriele, *Hildegard of Bingen*. Bear & Company, Sante Fe, New Mexico, 1983. In an age when it is easy to feel the wrath of God, Hildegard, living almost 900 years ago, would have us dare to feel God's pleasure.

Weems, Ann, *Kneeling in Jerusalem*. Westminster, John Knox Press, Louisville, Kentucky, 1992. Seventy-one poems of inspiration for use in the Lenten and Easter season.

Woodruff, Sue, *Mechtild of Magdeburg*. Bear & Company, Sante Fe, New Mexico, 1982. In moving drawings and well-chosen words from Mechtild, a 13th century mystic, we have a beautiful meditation experience based on God's wonderful creation, and humanity's dignity in God.

The Arms of the Diocese of Hamilton

The Coat of Arms of the Diocese of Hamilton was granted by the Crown in 1988. They are explained as follows:

The background of diamond shapes is a reference to the Arms of the Archdiocese of Toronto, from which the Diocese of Hamilton was divided. However, because each Diocese has its own history, the background differs in its arrangement from that of the Archdiocese. The background is meant to represent the diverse ethnic and national populations of the Diocese.

The Cross clearly identifies the Arms as being religious in nature.

In the upper left quadrant, the flower is meant to be the Mystical Rose. This is a reference to the Blessed Virgin as principal Patroness of the Diocese. It is crowned with a maple leaf crown, which refers to the titular of the Cathedral, Christ the King. The crown's maple leaves refer to the fact that we are a Canadian Diocese.

The flower in the lower right quadrant is called a cinquefoil, and is always present in a Coat of Arms for "Hamilton" (family, place, etc.). This same flower is found in the carpet and the stone work of the Cathedral.

The motto "Mater Viventium" (Mother of the Living) is taken from the Constitution on the Church of Vatican II, Chapter 8. It is used there in reference to Mary, and can also represent Holy Mother Church. Ultimately, the quotation is taken from the Greek Father of the Church, Saint Epiphanius.

The description of the Arms in heraldic terms is: Fusilly Gules and Argent overall a Cross Or in the first quarter a Rose Argent barbed and seeded Gold ensigned by a crown its finials of Maple Leaves also Gold and in the fourth quarter a Cinquefoil Ermine.

It is important to note that the Arms as granted are a patented trademark as of May 2, 1988. Thus, their use should not be authorized without the permission of the Bishop.

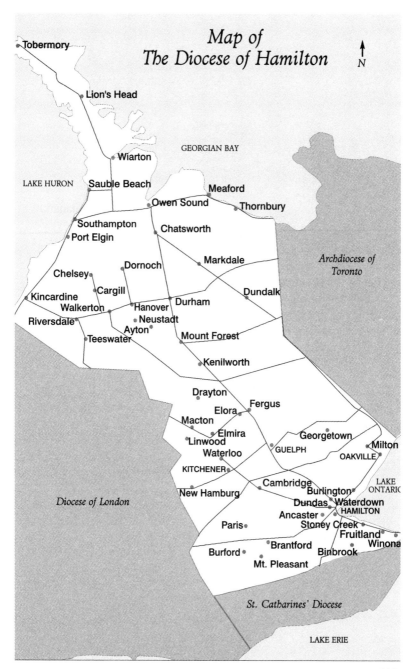

Map of
The Diocese of Hamilton

N

Tobermory

Lion's Head

GEORGIAN BAY

Wiarton

LAKE HURON   Sauble Beach

Meaford

Owen Sound

Thornbury

Southampton   Chatsworth
Port Elgin

Markdale

Chelsey   Dornoch

Archdiocese of
Toronto

Kincardine   Cargill
Walkerton   Hanover   Durham
Riversdale   Neustadt
Ayton
Teeswater   Mount Forest

Dundalk

Kenilworth

Drayton

Elora   Fergus

Macton

Elmira   Georgetown
Linwood   GUELPH   Milton
Waterloo   OAKVILLE

KITCHENER

Cambridge   LAKE ONTARIO
New Hamburg   Burlington
Dundas   Waterdown
Diocese of London   Ancaster   HAMILTON
Paris   Stoney Creek
Fruitland
Brantford   Winona
Burford   Binbrook
Mt. Pleasant

St. Catharines' Diocese

LAKE ERIE

113

OUR FAITH—FROM GENERATION TO GENERATION

Parishes of the Hamilton Diocese

Acton
St. Joseph   47 John Street South   (519) 853-0784

Ancaster
St. Ann   11 Wilson Street West   (905) 648-6874

Arthur
St. John   131 Georgina Street   (519) 848-2108

Brantford
Our Lady of Assumption   133 Murray Street   (519) 753-7316
St. Basil   50 Palace Street   (519) 752-0361
St. Joseph   235 Brant Street   (519) 752-2772
St. Pius X   9 Waverly Drive   (519) 753-8439

Burford
Blessed Sacrament   70 King St. W.   (519) 449-5143

Burlington
Holy Rosary   287 Plains Road East   (905) 634-7441
St. Adalbert   464 Plains Road West   (905) 523-1932
St. Gabriel   2261 Parkway Drive   (905) 336-7144
St. John the Baptist   2016 Blairholm Avenue   (905) 634-2485
St. Patrick   196 Kenwood Avenue   (905) 632-6114
St. Paul   2265 Headon Road   (905) 332-5115
St. Philippe   472 Locust Street   (905) 634-1743
St. Raphael   4072 New Street   (905) 637-2346

Cambridge
Our Lady of Fatima   185 Elgin Street   (519) 623-2320
St. Ambrose   210 South Street   (519) 621-2013
St. Clements   745 Duke Street   (519) 653-6123
St. Gregory   10 St. Gregorys Drive   (519) 623-3111
Sts. Martyrs Canadiens   71 Ainsley Street N.   (519) 622-4492
St. Mary   16 Cooper Street   (519) 658-4443
St. Patrick   53 Wellington Street   (519) 623-3773

Cape Croker   R.R.#5   (519) 534-3703

Carlsruhe
St. Francis Xavier   223 Concession 14   (519) 367-2693

Chepstow
Mary Immaculate   Concession Road 6   (519) 366-2353

Drayton
St. Martin of Tours   125 Union Street   (519) 638-2025

Dundalk
St. John Evangelist   271 Main St. E.   (519) 923-2042

Dundas
St. Augustine   58 Sydenham Street   (905) 628-2880

Durham
St. Peter   Highway 6   (519) 369-2605

Elmira
St. Teresa of Avila   19 Flamingo Drive   (519) 669-3387

Elora
St. Mary Immaculate   267 Geddes Street   (519) 846-5093

Erin
St. John de Brebeuf   24 Millwood Drive   (519) 833-9738

Fergus
St. Joseph   460 St. George Street West   (519) 843-5240

Formosa
Immaculate Conception   1 St. Ann Street   (519) 367-5341

Freelton
Our Lady of Mt. Carmel   79 Freelton Road   (905) 659-3305

Guelph
Holy Rosary   175 Emma Street   (519) 822-4701
Our Lady Immaculate   28 Norfolk Street   (519) 824-3951
Sacred Heart   75 Manitoba Street   (519) 844-8944
St. John   45 Victoria Road North   (519) 824-7311
St. Joseph   409 Paisley Road   (519) 822-4614

Halton Hills
Holy Cross   224 Maple Avenue   (905) 873-1887
Sacre Couer   39 Guelph Street   (905) 877-4373

Hamilton
Blessed Sacrament   305 East 37th Street   (905) 385-3570
Holy Cross   1883 King Street East   (905) 549-6707
Holy Family   1393 Cannon Street East   (905) 544-3146
Incarnation   400 Pottruff Road   (905) 561-7777
Notre Dame   132 Blake Street   (905) 545-6953
Our Lady of Lourdes   416 Mohawk Road East   (905) 383-3381
Sacred Heart   19 Viewpoint Avenue   (905) 383-3280
St. Ann   120 Sherman Avenue N.   (905) 544-0488
St. Anthony of Padua   165 Prospect Street N.   (905) 544-3327
St. Eugene   232 Queenston Road   (905) 549-2694
St. Gregory the Great   125 Centennial Parkway North   (905) 561-5971
St. John the Baptist   128 Edgemont Street S.   (905) 544-2100
St. Luke   200 Mount Albion Road   (905) 560-1551
St. Margaret Mary   20 Idlewood Avenue   (905) 388-2200
St. Patrick   440 King Street East   (905) 522-9828

Hamilton(Continued)

St. Peter Yu	6 Heath Street	(905) 545-3004
St. Stanislaus	8 St. Ann Street	(905) 544-0726
Cathedral	714 King Street West	(905) 522-5744
All Souls'	21 Barton Street West	(905) 528-1513
Annunciation	280 Limeridge Road West	(905) 388-2078
Canadian Martyrs	38 Emerson Street	(905) 528-4632
Corpus Christi	1694 Upper James Street	(905) 389-2474
Our Lady of Mercy	58 Dundurn Street North	(905) 522-5272
Regina Mundi	631 Mohawk Road West	(905) 385-3297
St. Boniface	327 Dundurn Street South	(905) 529-7902
St. Charles	129 Hughson Street South	(905) 528-0074
Sts. Cyril & Methodius	204 Park Street North	(905) 529-6674
St. Joseph	260 Herkimer Street	(905) 528-0019
St. Lawrence	475 Mary Street	(905) 522-6012
St. Mary	146 Park Street North	(905) 527-4216
Sts. Peter & Paul	50 Brucedale Avenue East	(905) 387-3550
St. Stephen	130 Barton Street East	(905) 529-1213

Hanover

Holy Family	352 Tenth Avenue	(519) 364-1973

Kenilworth

Sacred Heart	Highway 6	(519) 848-3210

Kincardine

St. Anthony	749 Russell Street	(519) 396-2505

Kitchener

Blessed Sacrament	305 Laurentian Drive	(519) 742-5061
Holy Family	180 Schweitzer Street	(519) 743-7121
Our Lady of Fatima	300 Simeon Street	(519) 894-4746
Our Lady of Guadalupe	79 Moore Avenue	(519) 744-4680
Sacred Heart	66 Shanley Street	(519) 742-5831
St. Aloysius	11 Traynor Avenue	(519) 893-1220
St. Anne	268 East Avenue	(519) 745-5302
St. Anthony Daniel	29 Midland Drive	(519) 893-6960
St. Francis of Assisi	49 Blueridge Avenue	(519) 745-7301
St. John	85 Strange Street	(519) 745-7855
St. Joseph	148 Madison Avenue South	(519) 745-9302
St. Mark	55 Driftwood Drive	(519) 571-9200
St. Mary	56 Duke Street West	(519) 576-3860
St. Teresa	44 Leonard Street	(519) 743-4525

Linwood

St. Mary	15 Isabella St. N.	(519) 698-2590

Markdale

St. Joseph	85 Toronto St.,	(519) 986-2192

Maryhill
St. Boniface   43 Church Street North   (519) 648-2069

Mildmay
Sacred Heart   2 Church Street   (510) 367-5304

Milton
Holy Rosary   139 Martin Street   (905) 878-6535

Mount Forest
St. Mary   230 Queen Street East   (519) 323-1054

New Hamburg
Holy Family   329 Huron Street   (519) 662-1744

Norval
Queen of Peace   9118 Winston Churchill Blvd.   (905) 456-3203

Oakville
Holy Trinity   2110 Trafalgar Road   (905) 842-2386
Mary Mother of God   463 Glenashton Drive   (905) 337-2184
St. Andrew   47 Reynolds Street   (905) 844-3303
St. Dominic   2415 Rebecca Street   (905) 827-2373
St. James   231 Morden Road   (905) 845-3603
St. Joseph   2028 Lumberman Lane   (905) 845-1364
St. Matthew   1125 Pilgrims Way   (905) 825-0219
St. Michael   282 Sewell Drive   (905) 844-7971

Owen Sound
St. Mary   554 - 15th Street East   (519) 376-0778

Paris
Sacred Heart   17 Washington Street   (519) 442-2465

Port Elgin
St. Joseph   920 Wellington Street   (519) 832-2202

Rockwood
Sacred Heart   232 Main Street   (519) 856-4711

Scotland
St. Anthony Daniel   57 Simcoe St.   (519) 446-2911

St. Agatha
St. Agatha   1839 Notre Dame Drive   (519) 747-1212

St. Clements
St. Clement   27 King Street West   (519) 699-4425

Stoney Creek
Assumption   63 Highway #20 East,   (905) 664-7651
Immaculate Heart   934 No. 8 Highway   (905) 643-1637
St. Francis Xavier   304 No. 8 Highway   (905) 662-8593

Teeswater		
Sacred Heart	14 Gordon Street	(519) 392-6935

Walkerton		
Sacred Heart	221 Victoria St.	(519) 881-0692

Waterdown		
St. Thomas	44 Flamboro St.	(905) 689-4857

Waterloo		
Our Lady of Lourdes	173 Lourdes St. West	(519) 886-0342
St. Agnes	75 Bluevale North	(519) 885-4480
St. Louis	53 Allan Street East	(519) 743-4101
St. Michael	240 Hemlock Street	(519) 884-9311

Missions

Mission	Parish
Ayr Catholic Community	Kitchener, Blessed Sacrament
Ayton, St. Peter	Carlsruhe, St. Francis Xavier
Brantford, Our Lady of Fatima	Brantford, Our Lady of the Assumption
Brantford, St. Theresa	Burford, Blessed Sacrament
Cargill, St. Joseph	Chepstow, Mary Immaculate
Chesley, St. Ann	Hanover, Holy Family
Chatsworth, St. Stanislaus	Owen Sound, St. Mary of the Assumption
Deemerton, St. Ignatius	Mildmay, Sacred Heart
Dornoch, St. Paul	Durham, St. Peter
Glenelg, St. John	Markdale, St. Joseph
Harriston, St. Thomas	Drayton, St. Martin of Tours
Hepworth, St. Mary	Owen Sound, St. Mary of the Assumption
Lions Head	Owen Sound, St. Mary of the Assumption
Macton, St. Joseph	Linwood, St. Mary
Meaford, St. Vincent	Owen Sound, St. Mary of the Assumption
Melancthon, St. Patrick	Dundalk, St. John the Evangelist
Milton, St. Peter	Milton, Holy Rosary
Milton, Our Lady of Victory	Milton, Holy Rosary
Neustadt, St. Joseph	Carlsruhe, St. Francis Xavier
Oustic, St. Peter	Rockwood, Sacred Heart
Palmerston, St. Mary Immaculate	Drayton, St. Martin of Tours
Saugeen, Sacred Heart	Cape Croker, St. Mary
Sauble Beach, Holy Family	Owen Sound, St. Mary of the Assumption
South Proton, St. Patrick	Dundalk, St. John the Evangelist
Southampton, St. Patrick	Port Elgin, St. Joseph
Tobermory, St. Thomas	Owen Sound, St. Mary of the Assumption
Wiarton, St. Thomas	Owen Sound, St. Mary of the Assumption

Acknowledgements

Design: Joe Smith,
                   St. Dominic Parish,
                   Oakville

Page 12   Beata Pytlik,
                   St. Francis of Assisi Parish,
                   Kitchener

Page 22   Vicky Tam,
                   Holy Rosary Parish,
                   Burlington

Page 38   Brian Tam,
                   Notre Dame Secondary School,
                   Burlington

Page 50   Sara Grégoire,
                   St. Thomas,
                   Waterdown

Page 66   Jeff Cross,
                   St. Mary Secondary School,
                   Owen Sound

Page 80   Sister Katherine Reiter,
                   School Sisters of Notre Dame,
                   Waterdown

Page 88   Grade 7/8,
                   Holy Rosary School,
                   Burlington

Page 114   John Nugent,
                   Our Lady of the Assumption,
                   Stoney Creek